Deeper?

Discovering an intimate relationship with God

Dr. Jacquelyn Hadnot

Deeper: *Discovering an intimate relationship with God*

Deeper: Discovering an Intimate Relationship with God
© Copyright 2012, Dr. Jacquelyn Brown-Hadnot
Kansas City, KS 66102

Unless otherwise indicated, all Scripture quotations are taken from King James Version of the Bible. Copyright © 2000 by AMG Publishers.

Scripture quotations marked AMP are taken from The Amplified Bible AMP. The Amplified Bible, Old Testament copyright © 1965, 1987 by the Zondervan Corporation. The Amplified New Testament, copyright © 1954, 1958, 1987 by the Lockman Foundation. Used by permission.

Please note that Igniting the Fire, Inc. publishing style capitalizes certain pronouns in Scripture that refer to the Father, Son, and Holy Spirit, and may differ from some Bible publishers' styles.

Published by Igniting the Fire, Inc.
1314 North 38th Street, Suite 102
Kansas City, KS 66102
www.ignitingthefire.net

Deeper: *Discovering an intimate relationship with God*

Table of Contents

Deeper: *Discovering an intimate relationship with God*

--𝒢ntroduction--

This booklet is dedicated to the women of the Intimate Encounters weekend. Special thanks to Lady Sandra Johnson for birthing Intimate Encounters. It is my prayer that God will ignite a fire within you to grow deeper in Him.

As you experience a new depth in God, I believe a deeper encounter will stir you to seek Him with a new intensity each day. Your prayer life will grow, and so will your worship. You will not look at worship the same way again. You will hunger

for more and your hearts desire will be to take worship deeper.

Enjoy the journey of growing deeper in the Lord. Grow deeper…

As the deer pants for the water brooks, so my soul pants for You, O God. My soul thirsts for God, for the living God.
Psalm 42:1-2

My soul follows hard after thee… Psalm 63:8

Chapter 1
God is calling us
deeper...

For years, God has kept me on my face, seeking His face in every aspect of my life and ministry. Often it seemed as if He kept me hidden from the world. Even with the books, cds, and radio and television ministry that He birthed through me, I still felt quiet from the world. I felt isolated as I waited to hear the purpose, plan and direction.

Knowing that He has a purpose and plan for my life, kept me in a place to hear Him. It kept me in a constant state of *"Go deeper because there is more that I require of you."*

God is calling us deeper. Deeper into His passion, deeper into His presence, deeper into the realm of the spirit that prepares us for the end times move of God.

Unfortunately, deeper is a place that many of us ask for, but in reality, we do not realize what we are asking. Deeper is a place that we must be prepared for. God in His loving and infinite wisdom knows that although we ask for deeper, many of us are not ready for it. He knows and gently nudges us in the direction of preparation.

God is ready to take a prepared people, deeper. He is ready to inhabit a prepared place. I am not speaking of a physical building; I am speaking of a prepared vessel. *"So as to make ready a people prepared for the Lord"* (Luke 1:17b).

We also must ensure that our church, ministry or home is conducive for a visitation by the Holy Spirit, while ensuring that we as the dwelling place is equally as prepared.

God wants to abide in His people. Often we are busy having church and we do not take the time to seek the Lord for the desires of His heart. We do not seek His face for the next move or direction. We are caught up in the hype of praise and leave God out. In other words, God is not abiding in many of our church services. If God is not abiding in our services, why are we having service? It is a dangerous thing to PRAISE the PRAISE and WORSHIP the WORSHIP. I hope you got that. We must praise and worship the creator NOT the creation.

As I sit putting pen to paper, the thought of God not abiding in me, with me and through me shakes the foundations of my heart. Apart from God, we can do nothing. If God is not abiding in us, it is impossible to go deeper. The Bible teaches us in John chapter 15 the need for abiding in the Lord. *"If you abide in Me, and My words abide in you, ask whatever you wish, and it will be done for you"* (John 15:7). It is time to abide in Him and go deeper. *Deep calls to deep...*

Chapter 2
Abide in Me?

"I am the true vine, and My Father is the vinedresser. "Every branch in Me that does not bear fruit, He takes away; and every branch that bears fruit, He prunes it so that it may bear more fruit. "You are already clean because of the word which I have spoken to you. "Abide in Me, and I in you. As the branch cannot bear fruit of itself unless it abides in the vine, so neither can you unless you abide in Me. "I am the vine, you are

the branches; he who abides in Me and I in him, he bears much fruit, for apart from Me you can do nothing. "If anyone does not abide in Me, he is thrown away as a branch and dries up; and they gather them, and cast them into the fire and they are burned. "If you abide in Me, and My words abide in you, ask whatever you wish, and it will be done for you. "My Father is glorified by this, that you bear much fruit, and so prove to be My disciples. "Just as the Father has loved Me, I have also loved you; abide in My love. "If you keep My commandments, you will abide in My love; just as I have kept My Father's commandments and abide in His love. "These things I have spoken to you so that My joy may be in you, and that your joy may be made full" (John 15:1-11).

The word abide means to *dwell or to live or reside in a place.* Therefore, God wants to dwell among His people. He wants to live or reside in us. Wow! God wants to take up residence in us. What an awesome thought, the Lord living in me, and working through me.

As wonderful as it sounds, ask yourself, am I ready for God to abide in me? Furthermore, am I ready to abide in God? There is a great price to pay when we are asking God to live in us. It means that no other spirit but the spirit of the Living God can rule our lives. We are saying to God, that we are ready to be pruned of the things that He deems a hindrance or an obstacle.

"Every branch in Me that does not bear fruit, He takes away; and every branch that bears fruit,

He prunes it so that it may bear more fruit."

Pruning is necessary so that He can remove weaknesses in us. Weaknesses such as fear, doubt, un-forgiveness, bitterness, lust, anger, etc. He also prunes us of religious spirits, personal agendas, pride and the like.

Here are seven points to consider when you ask God to abide in you:

1. **Source**: Jesus is the true vine. We must stay connected to him in order to bear fruit (v.1).

2. **Care**: God is the vinedresser. He cares for us (v. 2).

3. **Pruning**: God removes anything that hinders or weakens you (v. 2).

4. **Partners**: We are to bear fruit for the Lord (v. 4).

5. **Promise**: If we abide in Him and His word abides in us, He promises He will do what we ask (v. 7).

6. **Purpose**: Our purpose is to glorify God by bearing much fruit (v. 8).

7. **Obedience**: We must obey God. Abiding in Him means remaining in Him if we are to receive from Him and bear fruit for Him (v. 10).

Worship can be an intimate time between you and the Lord. It will be the place where He draws you near to Him. Draw near to God and He will draw near to you. Worship draws you closer to the Him and enables you to understand the seven points that you must consider what you ask Him to abide in you.

Abiding in Him always leads to worship. True worship leads to intimacy. Intimacy leads to divine fellowship with the One who first loved us. Therefore, we must understand the connection between intimacy, worship and abiding. It is important to understand that as you are seeking intimacy with the Lord - it will require a press.

Chapter 3
The Press for
Intimacy

Now that the foundation has been laid to help you understand the need to abide in God, let's press deeper into intimacy with God. Without the desire to abide in Him, there will be no intimacy with Him. Intimacy and abiding go hand in hand. You cannot have one without the other.

Intimacy is defined as:

- Close relationship: a close personal relationship.
- Quiet atmosphere: a quiet and private atmosphere.
- Detailed knowledge: a detailed knowledge resulting from a close or long association or study.

When you have a close personal relationship with someone, you are concerned with what pleases them, their likes, dislikes, and their overall well-being. In addition, you will set aside quality time or quiet time to be with them. Finally, you have knowledge of them, which only comes from a close or long association. The same way with God, when you are intimate with God your relationship carries all the same attributes.

I ascribe to the word "passionate" when I

describe my relationship with the Lord. It is as "passionate" as it is limitless. It is as limitless as it is fulfilling. It is as fulfilling as it is deep. The relationship you have with the Lord should not be contained within the confines of the church. Your relationship with Him MUST transcend all boundaries because it should be as infinite as the Infinite One.

How do you obtain intimacy with God? Through worship and prayer. Worship is the key that unlocks an intimate relationship with Him. True worship is God-centered not self-centered. When we take the focus off God, we stray in our focal point and tend to be focused on where we should worship, what music we should sing, and how the worship looks to other people. Focusing on these things completely misses the point and it is not true worship. Jesus tells us that true worshipers will worship God in spirit and in truth (John 4:24).

It is vital to your growth that you understand true worship and the impact true worship has on every aspect of your spiritual life. If we are to grow in the Lord, we must understand what we are presenting to the Lord. Remember, your relationship depends on it.

Chapter 4
Present Your Body
for Worship

There is the motivation to worship *"the mercies of God"* (Romans 12:1-2). God's mercies consist of everything He has given us that we don't deserve: eternal love, eternal grace, the Holy Spirit, peace, joy, faith, comfort, strength, wisdom, hope, patience, kindness, righteousness, security, eternal life, forgiveness, reconciliation, justification, sanctification, freedom, and much more. When we understand the extraordinary gifts that Father has in store for us, we should be motivated to pour out praise and thanksgiving—in other words, we should desire to worship!

Here is a description of the manner of our worship: "*present your bodies a living and holy sacrifice.*" Presenting our bodies means giving God our all. The reference to our bodies means all our human capabilities, our hearts, minds, thoughts, attitudes. In other words, we are to give up control of these things and turn them over to Him. I am sure you are asking how? "By the renewing of your mind." We renew our minds daily by cleansing ourselves of the world's "wisdom" and replacing it with true wisdom that comes from God. We must avoid the traditions of man and the rudiments of this world. Traditions are *long-established actions or patterns of behavior in a community or group of people, often ones that have been passed down from generation to generation.* Rudiments include *the basic principles or elementary teachings of this world* rather than on the teachings of Christ. "See to it that no one carries you off as spoil or makes you yourselves captive by his so-called philosophy and intellectualism and vain deceit (idle fancies and plain nonsense), following human tradition (men's ideas of the material rather than the spiritual world), just crude notions following the rudimentary and elemental teachings of the universe and disregarding [the teachings of] Christ (the Messiah) (Colossians 2:8 AMP). Renew your mind through the Word of God.

As the deer pants for the water brooks, so my soul pants for You, O God. My soul thirsts for God, for the living God (Psalm 42:1-2). Are you thirsty for His touch? Psalm 63:8 tells us that *my soul follows hard after thee*. Are you in pursuit of a love relationship with Him?

I pray that this short teaching will get you jump-started on the road to an intimate love relationship with the Lord. Your journey of discovering a passion for His presence will not be denied. When you seek Him, you will find Him.

There is a song on my CD The Extravagant Love of God entitled, *Deeper*. It speaks of the journey of going deeper into the presence of the Lord. *Enjoy the journey into deeper...*

Chapter 5
Deeper...

Deeper in you, I want to go deeper in you.

My soul longs to go deeper. My heart,

mind, cry deeper, into you.

The song "Deeper" opens with a soothing healing guitar and the Songbird, Zenobia Smith crying out from a place of longing and worship, she cries out for deeper as if her life depended on it.

When God wrote "Deeper" through me it was during a time when I was searching for a deeper place in Him. My heart, mind and body wanted more. As worshippers we are always searching for *that place* in God where we can see the manifested glory of God. Surface worship is not enough, we want more. Dr Margaret Wright wrote in the Foreword to the book, *The Extravagant Love of God*, "The entire body of Christ is yearning for a deeper encounter with the Spirit of God. This is the time when our Lord is awakening the deep love for Him that has been dormant too long." She is right, people are longing for more of God, but they don't know how to attain it. They are tired on living of the surface, eating the crumbs of stale bread. They are told that there is bread in the house, but when they open the "spiritual oven" they find that the oven is cold and there is no bread in the house of God. Stale bread and re-hydrated worship mean hungry worshipers longing for more of God, longing for deeper...

Without a hunger for more of God, we will grow stale and lukewarm. We will stop pressing into His presence and we will eventually stop growing in the things of God. Our preaching, teaching, music, worship - become stale and lack the intimacy needed to flourish in God. In other words, you loose your strength.

Your Strength Lies In Deeper...

Your strength lies deeply rooted in your prayer life. Your daily chase needs to be in a realm that flows like a river. But you must press into prayer with an intensity that is in harmony with your passion for His presence. It cannot be a hit or miss prayer life. Deeper will not come with hit or miss encounters. When you press in with an intensity that is consistent your hunger, you will find ALL your answers, your breakthrough and your release.

Growing Deeper

The Lord desires to use the elements of your past and present to take you to another level in Him. We should not allow the past or the present to hinder our growth. It is through the trying or trials of our faith that we are made stronger and wiser. *"That the trial of your faith, being much more precious than of gold that perisheth, though it be tried with fire, might be found unto praise and honour and glory at the appearing of Jesus Christ"* (1 Peter 1:7).

We are soldiers for Christ and if we are to stand for what is right, avoid playing games and run the race in an uncompromising stance - we will come to realize that although the adversities of life will try to overtake us, *NO weapon formed against us shall prosper.* The Word of God did not say it would not form, the Word of God says it will not prosper in your life.

As we go through, we must know that worship is our best weapon in the midst of the warfare. Ninjas have stealth like moves; armies have guns; and believers have worship. It is through our worship that our victory is sure. The enemy often looks like he is winning, never the less, *NO weapon formed against you shall prosper.* The enemy will try to discourage worship in order to keep you out of the presence of God. It is in the presence of the Lord that you will find peace, joy, love, contentment, victory and answers to your questions.

If we are to live a victorious life and experience the extravagance of God's love, we must address our spiritual priorities. In order to experience the extravagance of His love we must learn to walk in victory. Learning to walk in victory means that we address key issues that affect our focus, faith, and source of power. Without the proper focus, we will continually get off course. I refuse to be a victim in any aspect of my life. The Lord calls us to be victors through the blood of the Lamb of God. Therefore, we need to understand what elements shape a victorious life and the elements that lead us to defeat.

A victorious life says:

1. FOCUS: Lord Jesus Christ (John 14:6)
2. OBJECT OF FAITH: The Cross of Christ (Romans 6:3-5)
3. POWER SOURCE: Holy Spirit (Romans 8:1-2, 11)
4. RESULTS: Victory (Romans 6:14)

It would be unfair to give you the positive side of a victorious life and omit the way most believers live:

1. FOCUS: Works
2. OBJECT OF FAITH: Performance
3. POWER SOURCE: Self
4. RESULTS: Defeat

➢ Are you focused on the Lord or your works for the Lord?

➢ Is the object of your faith the Cross of Christ or how you perform for Christ?

➢ Is your power source the Holy Spirit or your *self-spirit*?

➢ What are the results of your efforts in life: victory or defeat?

In taking a spiritual inventory of your lifestyle, you will be able to see if you are walking in victory or defeat. If you can answer yes to any of the next questions, it will be a major step in discovering who God meant for you to be. Are you living a victorious life? Are you experiencing the extravagance or the fullness of God's blessings? Do you experience the *"I don't know why God is not blessing me"* blues?

II Chronicles 7:14-15 tells us, *"If my people, who*

are called by my name, will humble themselves and pray and seek my face and turn from their wicked ways, then will I hear from heaven and will forgive their sin and will heal their land. Now my eyes will be open and my ears attentive to the prayers offered in this place." We must be in a position of humility and obedience to the Lord if we are to receive His blessings. Unfortunately, believers often think that simply being "saved" is enough to receive the blessings of God. This misconception will leave them empty, disillusioned and in some instances angry with God. They don't realize that there are conditions that must be met in order to be in position to receive from God. God is not a "sugar daddy" or "magic lamp" that you rub when you want a "wish" or blessing. You must meet the conditions to be blessed.

Take a look at several steps that will help you move toward a deeper more intimate relationship with the Lord. These elements will help you move into position to be blessed.

- ➤ **Return to God** - We must humble ourselves, pray and seek the face of God. (II Chron 7:14)

- ➤ **Have faith in God** - Our faith should be simple and pure, like the attitude of a child.

- ➤ **Fear not** - God has not given us the spirit of fear, but of power, love and a sound mind. (2 Timothy 1:7)

- ➤ **Put on the full armor of God** - Be strong with the Lord's mighty power. (Ephesians 6:10-18)

- ➤ **God's call for intimacy** - God is calling us to intimacy with Him.

➤ **Worship** - Worship God in Spirit and Truth. Glorifying Him with a heart that's pure. (Psalm 51:10; John 4:23-24)

➤ **Give glory to God** - He is glorified through His creation, His son Jesus, and believers who are living for Him. Give God Glory in all that you do.

➤ **Find joy in everyday life** - Whenever trouble comes your way, let it be an opportunity for joy. The joy of the Lord is your strength. (Nehemiah 8:10)

➤ **Pass your test** - When your faith is tested, your endurance grows. (1Peter 1:7)

➤ **Know that God is in control** - God is in control and He loves you. He knows what's best for you. (Jeremiah 29:11)

➢ **Trust God** - Trust in God's plan for your life. (Proverbs 3:5)

Deep calls unto deep. The depths of the true and living God are calling us to a deeper place in Him. *As the deer pants for the water brooks, so my soul pants for You, O God. My soul thirsts for God, for the living God.*

Several years ago as I was preparing for bed the Lord spoke these words to me. He said, *"The reason you have the relationship with me that you do is because you have chosen to live a life for me. Few people desire to live at this level. This is why I speak to you. It is not a light thing, but it is not deep enough, go deeper."* Since that day I have been pressing in to deeper. It is not a light thing and it is not an easy thing. *Deeper* has required a sacrifice unlike any other in my life.

In order to go deeper, it will require sacrifice. The Word of the Lord, "Do you see the enemy trying to hinder My people as they move into position to advance towards their due season?"[1]

The answer is - yes. Throughout my travels, teaching, counseling and the like, I have met people who were caught in the tricks, traps and snares of the enemy. They got so caught up in the things that the enemy threw at them, they could not see God. The enemy became their primary focus and they lost sight of God. They became Satan conscious and not God conscious. Their entire life became engulfed in the attacks of the enemy. They resorted to praying their problems and thus gave the victory and the glory

---

[1] Dr. Jacquelyn Hadnot, The Extravagant Love of God: Experiencing the Prophetic Flow of God, 2010

to the enemy.

Wars have many battles, battles where victory is attributed to the enemy. The trials of our faith are precious to God. They are precious when we are able to stand unmovable and unshakable on His promises. He promised to never leave us nor forsake us. He promised that we are more than conquerors. He promised that we are over comers by the Blood of the Lamb. He promised that He would not withhold any good thing if we walked upright before Him. There are thousands of promises in the Word of God. Surely, we can grab hold of at least one of them and HOLD ON!

If you want more of God - go deeper.

If you want more from God - go deeper.

If you want more peace - go deeper.

If you want healing - go deeper.

If you want deliverance - go deeper.

Deeper: *Discovering an intimate relationship with God*

If you want joy - go deeper.

If you need hope - go deeper.

If you want freedom - go deeper.

If you want strength from God - go deeper.

If you want the fullness of God - go deeper.

If you want growth - go deeper.

If you want more - go deeper.

As you grow deeper in the Lord, allow Him to move you to another level, realm or dimension at His pace. Moving at His pace will ensure that you are in step with His plan for your life. It will also ensure that you don't miss Him and become prey for the enemy.

As we will grow in God, He will strengthen us. With each step we take, He will strengthen our spiritual legs and "make our feet like hinds' feet, and sets us upon high places" (Psalm 18:33 paraphrased). The Lord is ready to establish you in the places of your destiny. He is ready to set you on the course for greater and deeper. Are you ready? It's time to grow deeper.

Let today be the day that you begin to press in to deeper...

Deeper: *Discovering an intimate relationship with God*

Grow Deeper!

Live Deeper!

Love Deeper!

Deeper...

Deeper...

Deeper...

Deeper: *Discovering an intimate relationship with God*

My soul longs

to go

Deeper...

My heart, my

mind, cry for

Deeper...

Deeper: *Discovering an intimate relationship with God*

... For my soul follows hard after thee.

About the Author...

God has called Jacquie Hadnot to encourage, inspire, motivate and activate the gifts of the Spirit in order to raise powerful ministries in the body of Christ. She is becoming a voice on the subject of prayer, worship and spiritual warfare.

She is recognized as a modern-day apostle with a strong prophetic and psalmist anointing. She has a revelational teaching ministry with a mandate to saturate the world with the Word of God. Jacquie's heart is to see people arise and walk in the destiny and inheritance of the Lord.

She founded and established It Is Written Ministries, a publication company, an accounting and consulting firm, and a global radio station.

As a retired accountant and financial executive, Jacquie blends ministerial and entrepreneurial applications in her ministry to enrich and empower a diverse audience with skills and abilities to take kingdoms for the Lord Jesus Christ. A lecturer, conference speaker, teacher, business trainer, and financial consultant, she provides consulting services to businesses, churches, and individuals. She has written over twenty-five books, manuals, and other materials on intimacy with God, prayer, fasting and spiritual warfare. She has also released several music Cds and received numerous music and book publishing awards.

Beyond the pulpit, Jacquie is a talk-show host on both television and radio with her own program, Light for Your Path. Weekly she applies God's wisdom to today's world solutions. Her ministry goal is to make Christ's teachings relevant for today. She also publishes a quarterly magazine by the same name.

In addition to her vast experience, Jacquie has a Thd. in Pastoral Theology and a Masters in Ministry Leadership. She is also a wife, mother of one daughter and grandmother of one grandson. She and her husband, Gregory presently pastor It Is Written Ministries in Kansas City Kansas. They also serve as owners and officers of Igniting the Fire Media Group.

Worship is her passion...

For more on Apostle Jacquie please visit her website at www.jacquiehadnot.com.

Deeper: *Discovering an intimate relationship with God*

Other Books & Materials by Dr. Jacquie

Books in Print

- The Art of Spiritual Warfare (2012) (Book & Journal)
- A Woman of Worth: Loving the Skin I'm In (Book & Journal)
- A Woman of Worth: Loving the Skin I'm In Study Guide
- A Woman of Worth: From Victim to Victor
- A Woman of Worth: Dressed to Heal (Book & Journal)
- Closing the Doors to Satan's Attacks: *Overcoming Fear*
- Trapped in the Arms of Death: *Overcoming Grip of Suicide*
- Your Declaration of Dependence on God
- In the Face of Adversity: *Overcoming Life's Storms*
- The Enemy in Me: *Overcoming Self-Life Issues*
- There's a Famine in the Land: *Overcoming the Great Recession*
- Ignite My Fire, Lord (Book & Journal)
- The Extravagant Love of God: Experiencing the Prophetic Flow
- Cry Aloud, Spare Not! A Prophetic Call to the Fast
- Cry Aloud, Spare Not! The Companion-Study Guide
- Standing for the King: While in the Spotlight of the Media
- Pretty in Pink: Praying Influential Nonsense Free Women
- Unlocking the Power to Get Wealth
- His Mercy Endures Forever: Psalms, Prayers & Meditations
- To Make War with the Saints: Satan's Kingdom Agenda
- A Treasure in the Pleasure of Loving God
- Loving God through His Names: 365 Days of the Year
- When Fear Crept In

Deeper: *Discovering an intimate relationship with God*

- Deeper...
- Naked, Broken and Unashamed
- Where Is Your God? Have We Lost the Referential Fear of the Lord? (Coming 2014)

Audio Books & Teachings
- More of You... (Volume 1)
- In the Face of Adversity: *Overcoming Life's Storms*
- Be Not Deceived...
- Where Is Your God?
- Recognizing Your Due Season
- Praying the Healing Scriptures
- The Enemy in Me: *Overcoming Self-Life Issues*
- Trusting God in a Season of Discouragement
- The Harlot Heart

Journals
- Be Still and Know that I am God
- More of You
- Diary of a Psalmist

Music
- The Extravagant Love of God
- The Spoken Word of Love
- His Mercy Endures Forever: Praying the Psalms

Deeper: *Discovering an intimate relationship with God*

DVD

- ➤ When Your Faith is Being Tested
- ➤ What Made David Run
- ➤ Agents of Change
- ➤ Virtuous Women of Worship

Books in Print - Over comers Series

- ➤ Closing the Doors to Satan's Attacks: *Overcoming Fear*
- ➤ Trapped in the Arms of Death: *Overcoming Grip of Suicide*
- ➤ In the Face of Adversity: *Overcoming Life's Storms*
- ➤ The Enemy in Me: *Overcoming Self-Life Issues*
- ➤ There's a Famine in the Land: *Overcoming the Great Depression*

TO CONTACT DR. JACQUIE:
www.jacquiehadnot.com
www.ignitingthefire.net
Or write us:
jacquie@jacquiehadnot.com

Deeper: *Discovering an intimate relationship with God*

www.ingramcontent.com/pod-product-compliance
Lightning Source LLC
Chambersburg PA
CBHW060618030426
42337CB00018B/3106